THE UNTOLD STORY

Live with Your Regrets, Die with Your
Dreams or Choose to Walk in Your Awesomeness!

Catrina M. Wilson
and
Twana Y. Wilson

DISCLAIMER AND LIMIT OF LIABILITY: This book details the author's personal and professional experiences with and opinions about job and business-related matters. While the information in this book may be found to be useful, the authors and publisher make no claim to be licensed as a teacher, psychologist, or psychiatrist, or any other profession that would engage in presenting career, legal, emotional, financial, relationship, or health advice. The author and publisher are providing this book and its contents on an "as is" basis and make no representations or warranties of any kind with respect to this book or its contents. Except as specifically stated in this book, neither the author or publisher, nor any authors, contributors, or other representatives will be liable for damages arising out of or in connection with the use of this book. This is a comprehensive limitation of liability that applies to all damages of any kind, including (without limitation) compensatory; direct, indirect or consequential damages; loss of data, income or profit; loss of or damage to property and claims of third parties. You understand that this book is not intended as a substitute for consultation with a licensed medical, educational, legal or accounting professional. Before you begin any change in your lifestyle in any way, you will consult a licensed professional to ensure that you are doing what's best for your situation. This book provides content related to educational topics, occupational strategies and transitions and entrepreneurship. As such, use of this book implies your acceptance of this disclaimer.

Table of Contents

This book is dedicated to:

My loving wife, Twana

You are my partner in life, my partner in business and sometimes my partner in crime. No one can begin to imagine all that we have been through in the 23 years (and counting) we've been together. I was there and I can hardly believe it. What I do know for certain is that we have been broke and broken, but the love we have for one another has never failed us. Despite our differences, the change in our circumstances, the emotional roller coaster ride, the ongoing distractions and the temporary setbacks, you have loved me unconditionally.

I have had many grandiose ideas, big dreams and insane goals and yet you have stood by and supported me. Thank you for being selfless in my pursuit of happiness, even though it has sometimes been at the expense of your own. You have made many sacrifices for the betterment of our lives and you have only wanted love in return. My heart is filled with so much admiration for the person you are. I am very blessed to have you in my life and be an extension of your family, as you are to mine. I promise you a lifetime of bliss and abundance.

I am extremely thankful that I have you to share in my vision and my story. I love you.
~ Yours Truly ~

My Other Half, Catrina

Despite all our flaws, imperfections and short-comings, we have withstood all of life's hills, dark alleys and steep mountains, continuously climbing, lighting up the darkness and accomplishing the most out of life. We started so young, barely out of our teenage years, with a child to raise, while we raised ourselves. Although we had the loving support of our families, it was just the two of us and we decided to stay '2gether-4ever.' "Young and dumb" as they say, we were never; we read a lot of books, asked many questions and had multiple aspirations to be better than our circumstances and never looked back. Now here we are.

You've continued to push through obstacles, remain sane during the most insane times and stayed true to your commitment to success. Our relationship, love and dedication have stretched beyond our imagination and with time, wisdom and growth, I cherish you in this new decade of our lives, unlike any other decade before. You are my beating heart, my life-mate and whole-heartedly, my other half.

To Our Son "Blest"

You look to us as your role models and you follow in our footsteps with so much gratitude. Fortunately, you were too young to remember some of our most horrific moments we shared together, although you have been through the storm with us. You have absorbed our strength and you are a beautiful reflection of the two moms, "your two queens" who raised you. You make us proud to call you our son. We turned the obstacles that have crossed our paths into opportunities to make us strong. Don't ever forget that. We have taught you, loved you and supported you. Stay true to yourself and you will forever be "Blest." We love you.

To Mom Deborah

Thank you love, for your impressive demonstration of motherhood. You are a walking billboard of strength and courage. Your kind heart, joyful spirit and optimism are infectious. You are a beautiful person inside and out and you are deserving of the best of what life has to offer. Thank you for being a praying mama; Lord only knows you have worn out some knee pads over the years. May you continue to be heavily blessed. We love you.

To Mom Brenda

You are the master of storytelling and we feel your spirit in the words of this book. We miss your sense of humor, your contagious laughter and your beautiful artwork. We know you are cookin' up something good in heaven and still making your famous cakes. We know how proud you must be of your "Pooch." May your soul be at peace in God's kingdom and may you feel our love with each passing day. Love you.

To God

Of course, our acknowledgments would be incomplete if we did not above all else, thank our heavenly father for his graciousness and generosity. God ~ we have learned how to be still and wait patiently as you continue to work miracles, create endless opportunities and shower us with blessings. Our existence and abundant life are possible because of you. We thank you for your unconditional love, ongoing support and for having a bigger vision and dream for us than we could ever have for ourselves. Your divine and powerful energy has continued to stir our soul, kept us humble, kept us grounded and kept our faith strong in some of our most challenging moments and we are forever grateful for all that you do.
~AMEN~

INTRODUCTION

One of our favorite of many quotes comes from Mark Twain: "The two most important days in your life are the day you are born, and the day you find out why." Sometimes, we have to be reminded that even within our dysfunction, our disorganized lives and our imperfections, we are perfect to play the role that was assigned to us. Despite our broken homes, broken hearts or broken history, we were born into this great world with a purpose to fulfill, and it is our obligation to complete the mission we were called to. Somewhere, deep down inside of every one of us, we know this to be the truth; we know it is our birthright to live abundantly, yet we disobey this right and disconnect from the magnitude of greatness that lies within us. We have the tendency to create a generational cycle of madness by scaling back on what we rightfully deserve and what is due to us. No one is exempt from abundance! It does not matter what color your skin is, or your level of education; nor does it matter your socioeconomic status or religious background. Regardless of your sexual orientation, or what zip code you were born in, you were born to do great things.

We convince ourselves that we are not good enough, lucky enough, rich enough, attractive enough, smart enough, worthy enough, strong enough, powerful enough or enough in many other ways. These are lies that we choose to tell ourselves and, with much conviction, we then believe. But these lies are wrapped up in fear and not faith; fear of the unknown, fear of the unfamiliar, fear of failure, fear of success, fear of power, fear of a new status, fear of entering an uncomfortable place, amongst many other fears. Fear can be superficial or can be buried in the deepest part of our subconscious mind. In either case, it is False Evidence Appearing Real, and if we give it power, it will immobilize us. We will stand by observing the rest of the world move through time. Fear is rooted in our existence; we utilize it as a coping mechanism and, particularly when we are in survival mode, we turn it on like a safety switch. However, not facing fear masks its presence, allowing it to persist, prolong its lifespan and not holding ourselves accountable exacerbates our discontent.

Perhaps your talents are multi-layered; therefore, you feel the need to do it all and are not sure where to focus. You end up the jack of all trades and master of none; could it be that you have the passion or know your purpose, but don't know how to develop it and incorporate it into your current situation? Maybe you aren't quite sure what it is you are born to do, or how to do it, or where to begin. Your purpose is that persistent calling that you repeatedly hear and cannot ignore and your passion is a thirst that drives you toward it; it takes the wheel even when you don't. Pay attention to the compliments people give you repeatedly. It might come in the form of a hobby that holds your interest more than any other, or it might simply start with one interest and that leads you to the talent or hobby that you are most passionate about.

Your life is no accident; it's no coincidence that you ended up exactly where you are today. However, the way you change your tomorrow is to get intentional about living the life that has been waiting to embrace you. Know this - there is no expiration date on your dreams except the one you put there!

Catrina's Story

We haven't gotten acquainted yet, but at first glance, it may seem to someone on the outside looking in that I am a well put-together individual. When people interact with me on a personal or professional level, they often evaluate what little they know about my life and title it as a success story, or someone living the good life. Considering my status in life today (an educated African-American woman with a few degrees under her belt who speaks articulately; dresses well; drives an expensive car; lives in a nice suburban neighborhood; an author and business owner; someone who has traveled extensively, has had some profound life experiences and is surrounded by a loving and supportive family), some might agree with this evaluation. It seems like an ideal description of the good life, but it just appears that way.

Although I come from a large and loving family, I was a very timid and an introverted child. I was raised by my mother who was a single parent, raising two, young, black girls in a very low-income neighborhood of Southeast San Diego. We lived in a neighborhood with such a bad reputation for drive-by shootings, gang bangers, and dope dealers, there was no such thing as pizza deliveries, and cops only frequented our neighborhood when they had ill-intentions. My mother, like most mothers in my neighborhood, was on government assistance, but it did not change our financial circumstances. I am so grateful that my mother smothered us with the riches of her love and I find comfort in knowing she did the best she could with the knowledge she had at the time.

Day after day, week after week, month after month and year after year, I watched my mother struggle to make ends meet, working jobs that paid her under the table and robbing Peter to pay Paul. It was common to eat breakfast foods for dinner and dinner for breakfast; we got creative with Top Ramen noodles (all 100 packs for $1!), and succotash was a household name. Now, that may sound like a fancy dish or gourmet meal to some of you, but in my house, it meant throwing in every single leftover from the fridge into the frying pan to make a meal. When it was my turn to go to the supermarket and get in line to pay for the food in the cart, I would let the entire store go before me because I was too embarrassed to use the book of food stamps my mother sent me to the store with.

My mother would invite her company to sit in her favorite green recliner. After they had gone, my sister and I would excitedly collect the loose change that fell from their pockets into the crevices of the recliner. We would save the coins and roll them up in coin rolls because that was one more meal we could depend on. And while I can laugh about it now, it was no laughing matter all those years ago.

I heard my mother's cries behind closed doors when she thought no one was listening and I saw the pain and disappointment in her eyes when she was not certain how she would provide for us. All around me were others like us: low-income families going through the same struggles, sharing the same stories and living the same reality. I soon realized the one thing we all had in common was the fact that no one was doing anything different. People were comfortable living in an uncomfortable situation, an all too familiar environment, even though they were repeatedly getting the same results. What I knew for sure, at a very early age, was that was NOT going to be my life, and I would have done just about whatever it took to make my reality look very different. I simply made up my mind that I would refuse to repeat the cycle that so many of us young, black children are subjected to, and that became my mission.

As my mother always taught me and my sister, the circumstances of our lives did not have to remain our reality or dictate our future. She taught us that choice would always be our greatest power and, of course, as most mothers do, she wanted us to have a better life than what she was able to provide for us. My mother, God bless her, planted seeds of hope and endless opportunities in our minds, even though our surroundings looked much different at the time; so, mediocrity and I never became friends. As far back as I can remember, I have always known I was here for something greater. In my younger years, I did not quite know how to articulate this into words. However, there was always a feeling there and a longing that remained with me no matter what path in life I had chosen. I promised myself that I would not become a product of the ghetto. I also vowed it would be the difference I made in my life that would be the change my mother would see in her life. That is where my transformation journey began and why I started being so goal-oriented and so career-driven. I was hungry for something different.

Life is the thing that happens as we are making plans. Although I worked relentlessly to make a better life for myself, before all of my achievements and accomplishments, I ended up living the very life I attempted to run from. I moved out of my mother's house at 17 years old. My mother and I were best friends, but I always had an independent spirit, and by that age, I wanted to do things my way. That was never going to happen under my mother's roof. I didn't move very far, just right across the street actually, but it was a start, and an exhilarating feeling, I might add. However, instead of living in an area that was somewhat hidden from the ongoing activity of "the hood," my apartment faced the street, so I had a view of just about every incident that occurred. It was very bothersome to repeatedly be an eyewitness to the gang violence, the prostitution, the neglected and abused children, the drug dealer's hustle, the crackhead's struggle, the disrespectful 'brothas' I walked past daily on the street corners while they yelled obscenities to every "shorty" on the block, the young girls pregnant with their third child, unable to take care of the two they already had, those who made it a full-time job to milk the system, rather than get off their lazy butts and work for a living, giving a bad reputation to those who really needed the assistance of welfare. Frankly, I was tired of being constantly reminded that while there was so much movement going on in the city streets, at the end of the day, there was no movement at all.

Two years had passed, and I could no longer tolerate the behaviors I just described. Fortunately, by 19 years old, I landed my first "real job" in corporate. I was hired as a PBX Operator for a manufacturing company and eventually started on-the-job training in the accounting department. Once I became proficient in this area, I got promoted and did taxes on the side for extra cash. When money was tight, I would make quick cash working telemarketing positions and, in the summer months, I worked part-time at a non-profit organization that served high-risk youth. This afforded me a move to "Paradise Hills," a much nicer area in San Diego, just 10 minutes away from mom. However, as my career-life was improving, other areas in my life suffered. Between the ages of 17 and 23, life was throwing punches and curve balls left and right. Dodging those punches and curve balls became increasingly difficult. I was drowning financially, so I swallowed my pride and attempted to get some government assistance (just an EBT card for food) and was declined due to "not being far enough below the poverty line." I ended up a single mom with high credit card debt and a lot of baggage that I couldn't seem to get rid of, despite my desperate ongoing efforts. I was devastated that the end result of my years of hard work and dedication ended me up there (an all too familiar place). I decided to start an anonymous life out of state with the plan to provide a healthy lifestyle for myself and my son, who now depended on me. As you can imagine, this changed the trajectory of my life.

Needless to say, my priorities were drastically altered and over the course of the subsequent years, I found myself depressed, distressed and not quite in the position academically, emotionally or financially I had once anticipated. As a result, I started living job to job, paycheck to paycheck and I was extremely unhappy feeling stuck in this cycle, but it was what I was most familiar with. By 23 years old, I was very blessed to have gotten into a relationship with my female life partner who significantly contributed to our household, livelihood, and motherhood in every way imaginable. However, together with our obligations being so great at such a young age, we were barely making it, going from pawnshops between paychecks and, at our lowest point, when we had no one and nowhere to turn for help, we shamefully stole food from the supermarket just to survive. We risked going through the checkout line to pay for the items we could afford and shoved the items we couldn't afford in inconspicuous places (inside our purses, pants, and pockets). While our hearts pounded through our chest a mile per minute and our nerves were on end, we silently prayed to God that we didn't get caught and asked for forgiveness. We made a promise to create a plan B and never return to that dreadful place ever again. We never did.

Twana's Story

I am the only one in my immediate family to graduate high school, further my education with a higher degree, serve in the military, move across country (almost 3,000 miles away from my family), travel the world, own businesses and make smart investments. However, by no means have I been confident, self-assured and a picture of strength in the way that I carried myself. Just the opposite: I was quite shy and, unlike Catrina, grew up in a two-parent household, in a nice neighborhood in Queens, New York, along with my older sister. I had a memorable and enjoyable childhood. My mom and dad kept food on the table, a roof over our heads and clothes on our backs. My mom was a bright light and found a unique way to take someone out of the most traumatic of events and without warning have them laughing hysterically, causing them to forget their pain in that moment. She filled the room with love and laughter in any situation; her storytelling and sense of humor were infectious. Her creative cooking, strong work ethic and craftmaking abilities were a true reflection of the beauty she possessed within. Whereas, my dad, was simply one of the hardest working men I had ever known and very strict. He also knew his way around the kitchen and had a really good sense of humor as well. The combination aided in our home being filled with continuous joy in spite of all life's challenges.

I had no idea that we were struggling financially until one night my mother told my sister and me to get dressed, grab a bucket and follow her across the street to the fire hydrant. In her hand, she had a large wrench, which she used to turn on the water and we each started filling our buckets to a level that was manageable for us to carry. My mother would use small amounts at a time for a bath, reserving some water to cook with and to flush the toilet. Even through that experience, I did not know that we were classified as poor because everyone around me lived in this manner. In my mind, the Ethiopian children we saw on television with flies surrounding them and the advertisements that urged families to send money ("just one dollar per day will feed a family for a year") were considered poor.

Although growing up in Queens had a lot to offer, including family and friends, my parents made the decision to move down South. I quickly learned and had my first experience with racial discrimination. When I was fourteen years old, my mom and I went to the local doctor in a town called North, South Carolina (I know, the name of the town is confusing) and to our surprise, we had to enter the doctor's office on the side of the building marked "colored." One of my first summer jobs was to help my grandmother (my mother's mother) pick peanuts for five dollars per bushel (approximately 3 feet high). Aside from the KKK rallies in the middle of town, the confederate flag flying proudly atop the state capital building, the outrageous bumper stickers and the in-your-face attitude from white folk, I found the town of North to be quite charming, and the southern hospitality in the African-American community was heartfelt. The town folk waved every single time I drove by, no matter how many times per day I drove by. This was my first introduction to Southern hospitality.

However, I grew quite weary of the slow pace, the unobjectionable mindset of the South, the yes ma'am/no sir mentality and the prominent bigotry, so I decided to join the military. College was not the answer for me at the time. In 1988, I traveled across the country to sunny

California, and the military broadened my horizons, as I had the opportunity to meet people from around the globe. I enjoyed my freedom, my new military family, and the life that Southern California offered. However, the dream was short-lived: I was asked by one of my male military counterparts why I had joined the navy. Before I could formulate my response, he sarcastically said, "Didn't you want to stay home, find a husband and have babies?" It was the first time I realized and was a witness to the anger and resentment that many military men so strongly felt about women serving in the military. Not only were women being allowed in the military, but they were starting to join and show up in record numbers. Military men could not comprehend nor appreciate equal rights in that particular environment; it was as if the enemy had invaded their territory. It was at this point that I knew for sure the military would not be a long-term endeavor for me.

Catrina and I met in 1993 and formed a union a year later in 1994. Together we had a lot of big dreams and goals with regards to doing well for ourselves and helping our families to succeed as well and to educate and give back to our communities. However, we knew it would take money to make money, and at the time, although we had brilliant ideas that flowed in abundance, money was still quite scarce. A roommate situation gone bad caused an unfortunate and abrupt ending of a long-term friendship, leaving my new family and me without the necessities (little to no food, utilities were shut off without warning, and our shelter was threatened with a 10-day eviction notice). As the sole provider, I had to think very quickly about what our next move would be. I did not have much time to make a decision, and with a shortage of funds, our choices were extremely limited as far as what we could afford. So, we had to leave our cozy 2-bedroom apartment to move into a mobile home community, a trailer park, where our mobile home sat empty, surrounded by numerous other mobile homes, many of which were not well-maintained. That was definitely a huge adjustment.

We had to start over, because the few valuable items we owned, such as an old television set, a couple of low-quality furniture pieces and some jewelry that didn't have much (if any) value, had to be sold so we could get quick cash. I was working as an armed security guard at the time, and it paid minimum wage, which was $6.50 per hour. That did not provide much for a family of three regardless of how much overtime I worked. Thankfully, my position was stationed at an upscale cardiovascular facility that planned events on a frequent and routine basis. The expensive food and drinks they were ready to dispose of became a meal for my family. It was also a place to get warm during the cold winter months and, if necessary, it offered clean showers with running hot water. We were so grateful to have a mutual friend who was caring enough, despite her battle with substance abuse, to invite us to a local restaurant she managed, where she fed us a hearty meal on the house and packed us extra food to go when she could do so without getting caught. Otherwise, we went without food, so our son had enough to eat. Special occasions didn't feel so special; especially during the holiday season. Our Charlie Brown Christmas tree was bare, with only two to three gifts underneath it sent from family members, not gifts we bought for one another. Rationing food portions during an already restricted Thanksgiving dinner was our unfortunate reality. Birthday celebrations and holidays were typically intimate, quality time spent with one another. We learned to be resourceful and appreciate the love instead of focusing on the lack.

Ironically, Catrina and I have always been the go-to people for advice and financial assistance for our family and friends. Obviously, we didn't have much to offer, but there was something so reflective in us that allowed people to see the betterment of their own lives. We didn't necessarily see it in ourselves, yet when we delivered the message or shared our story, not only was it well received, it was one of the most rewarding tasks we had ever experienced. The seed was planted early in our minds that we could become influential leaders and a trusted source because what little we had in comparison to the progress we had been making to turn our lives around held people's interest. They needed to know how we did it and we were always happy to share. This was our AHA moment - most definitely our turning point.

Brainwashed, Broke and Broken

Fast forward to the 21st century. We quickly got our lives together. We took the advice of our parents, who taught us what their parents and society taught them which is to go to school and get a high school diploma, go to college and get a degree, get a good job, and climb the ladder. They wanted us to teach the same principles to our children so they can repeat the cycle, and everyone can live happily ever after. Sound familiar?

Well, because the seeds were planted early, we worked in corporate, while climbing the ladder and operating our businesses on the side. By 2005, we owned multiple real estate properties, and by the end of 2006, we had our grand opening for our clothing line. However, when the market crashed, we were ill-prepared, as was the majority of the nation, and it had a domino effect on our lives. We had to short-sale our primary residence, as well as one of our investment homes and were forced into foreclosure on the other investment home. Therefore, we had to cease sales with the clothing line because we had no money to invest back into the business, nor did we have time to market properly. Needless to say, we had to humbly go back into the corporate workforce and work harder than ever to regain stability.

We did all of the above and, as it turns out, we were extremely miserable. After it was all said and done, we did not feel satisfied, nor did we feel as though we were living our most authentic lives. When you start looking forward to Friday on Monday morning and calling the boss into your office, you know it's time to go! We followed society's protocol and went to college. A few degrees later and with the alphabet soup of credentials behind our names, we ended up with debt and dead-end jobs that did not promise job security or job satisfaction. In fact, we've since had experiences related to employment that aided in our turning point. In short, we decided to temporarily relocate from Murrieta, California to Atlanta, Georgia to be closer to our family on the East Coast. The timing couldn't have been more perfect; we had saved a significant amount of money and were ready for a change. Atlanta seemed to be a place of opportunities, specifically for women of color. Considering our skill set and educational background, we had no reason to doubt the flood of job prospects.

After six months of being rejected for one reason or another and depleting our available funds, we realized how wrong we were and were sorely disappointed. It was a sobering moment. Apparently, we were disillusioned by what we thought our lives would look like. We decided to create a realistic opportunity and start our own business once again, one that we were solid with and passionate about. Of course, well into this lengthy process, we both landed a career opportunity. Although it was not the most ideal arrangement because we were working opposite schedules, we knew that it was only temporary. With that in mind, Catrina accepted a position with a well-known company that she would be able to transfer to upon her return to California, one that offered a great benefits package and a competitive salary. Twana accepted a position with a local and well-known company that gave her the experience she needed in the industry for which she worked, but the pay was low, and there was no benefit-package to compensate for that. Again, we saw this as a temporary investment.

Catrina, being protective by nature, found herself in a challenging situation that led her to stand firmly by her colleagues, repeatedly questioning and assertively pursuing answers, as it related to the potential compromise of patients' care and jeopardizing her RN license.

She was lead to believe she had the full support of her Director, yet she was terminated from the company only two months after her employment. The verbal reason given by the company was that she did not fit into the culture of the organization, but the written reason given specifically stated: "The needs of the position and Catrina's background are not in alignment." By the way, this termination came with an "ineligible to rehire" status. Infuriated and appalled at the way matters were handled, Catrina challenged the policies and involved key decision-makers to engage in an investigative process and address her concerns of wrongful termination based on retaliation. They claimed to have entertained her request, which lasted for approximately one month, but ultimately the employer did not budge from their decision, and there was nothing Catrina could do to change the outcome of that situation. There was no effective support system she could depend on and the individuals she stood by, stood up to and trusted deceived her. She ended up on unemployment and worked quickly to transition to self-employment, as she soon realized and eventually embraced that this was all happening for a good reason. What she thought was working against her, was actually working for her.

Twana's experience was different, but nevertheless, untimely and just as frustrating. After eight months with the company she was employed by, and because Catrina's employment situation had taken a sudden turn, Twana sought full-time employment opportunities internally and externally. Once realizing outside opportunities were not pouring in, she pursued positions within her company, and for months they gave her the run-around, during which time she continued to work per diem (aka PRN). Also, the only way she would qualify for more pay was by working a 10-hour night shift, where she would qualify for a shift differential. When the company was good and ready to offer her a full-time position, they wanted to hurry her through the hiring process with no remorse for not hiring her when she was in dire need.

So, the message in this is that we have repeatedly invested a great deal of time, money and energy with various employers, only to feel less fulfilled than ever. Enslaved by a modernized system that has continuously made us dance to their offbeat tune and yet, we found ourselves living our plan B rather than the life we were destined to live. By doing so, we felt as though we were betraying ourselves, dishonoring our ancestors who paved the way for our generation to have so much more out of life and doing the world a disservice by withholding information from individuals who could benefit from our experiences.

The truth is, like most people, we certainly endured our share of hardships, and we had more trauma, more drama, and more karma than the universal law should allow anyone in a lifetime. We started asking around, talking to strangers about equal rights, just in case someone out there was accepting donations for sob stories and pity parties. Unfortunately, we did not get any takers. We did realize how easy it is for the majority of us to get addicted to and trapped in our stories, our boxes, our bubbles, our fishbowls and our cages, even when it does not serve us well. Why? Because people allow themselves to be comfortable living in uncomfortable situations, rather than becoming uncomfortable and creating for themselves comfortable situations.

So, where did we go wrong? We bought into a brainwashed society and got stuck in a system that consistently fails us. We ignored our gifts and put them on the back burner while spending many years doing what we didn't love doing, ultimately leading to our discovery of what we did love doing. We had repeatedly heard but didn't listen, that "to get something different, you have to be willing to do something different," so we did. We simply could not continue to live the second phase of our lives repeating that cycle, so we chose a better path for ourselves and decided to re-write a different truth in the next chapters of our lives. How? We started with what we were familiar with and what we were talented with and felt our way from there. Considering we've always appreciated the power that words held, we thought of using our writing skills in combination with our creative skills to write greeting cards. In doing our research we learned that In Touch greeting cards (the name we chose for our product line) was already in existence and active, so we decided to go bigger and bolder.

We decided that T-shirts would be the canvas that would carry our words throughout the communities, peak interest and start a dialogue about controversial issues, heartfelt times and ultimately hold people accountable for their negative behaviors, so together we could eradicate them. That is how CaTwa Fitz came about. This concept was exciting and satisfying, but we wanted something more; we shared a much bigger vision, and we wanted to share in other women's visions just as we had done for years. That is when it occurred to us that we are overjoyed when we can help other women birth their vision into the world, hence the idea of Shared Visions By CaTwa (pronounced Kuh-Twah) being born.

Having worked a 9-5 since the age of 15 until the age of 45 (30 years!), we know a thing or two about not being content in the workforce. We had finally come to a crossroads in our career, with the awareness that we needed something more. It was no longer a matter of when rather a matter of what service we would devote ourselves to in the second phase of our lives that would bring with it a deeper level of gratification. After a lot of exploring, we chose the specialty area of helping wonderful women like you turn their lives around for the betterment of their immediate and far future and that of their children's; to find it within yourselves to dig deeper for the obvious answers that are already there; to love yourself enough that you would be willing to give yourself the greatest opportunity of a lifetime, one that the Divine Spirit has already granted you; to give yourself permission to fall in love with life by doing what you were created to do and to put your unique fingerprint on that which allows you to reach maximum heights with or without fear.

Get ready, get real and get radical! That means to be unstoppable, find ways around obstacles, jump hurdles and, most importantly, never give up on your dream and it won't give up on you. For us, that radical moment came at a time when unemployment paid us a visit; the primary source of income was a per diem job. All retirement funds had been withdrawn, and savings accounts were nearly depleted. There was no emergency fund or cash cushion to fall back on; credit cards were maxed out; a previous bankruptcy lingered on our credit reports, so we could not qualify for additional credit or do a balance transfer. We had already downsized to a small one-bedroom apartment with the bare necessities and significantly cut all expenses (cable TV, phones, internet services, pampering services, dining out), deferred school loans and made a dollar stretch for food. We had no family or friends to depend on, and opportunity wasn't knocking on our door. Guess what? We did it anyway and so can you. We are not telling you to do anything we wouldn't or already haven't done.

We at Shared Visions By CaTwa are here simply to guide you to what has been there all along. We want to help you connect your passion with your purpose and show you how to use your life experiences to share your story, produce a vision and get passionate about your message that others will relate to and benefit from. We will hold a mirror up to your beautiful face so that you can see your inner beauty radiate to your outer beauty. It is truly YOUR time to shine, to be the light in the darkness of others' lives and to bring hope for a brighter future. Your time is here TODAY and NOW! You cannot afford to miss out on the abundant life the universe has been waiting patiently to offer you. We help you discover and uncover your deepest aspirations. We are here to take your hand and walk with you, step-by-step, through the process of HOW to construct and sustain a successful business, which may feel like an intimidating journey, especially when you lack a strong support system. Allow us to be your personal mentors; your transformational coaches. Allow us to inspire, motivate and empower you to build a winning business around authenticity.

What This Book Can Do For You

This book will serve as a catalyst for change in the way our minds are conditioned in a brain-washed society. It primarily speaks to aspiring women entrepreneurs who want to attain and sustain a life of entitled fulfillment, yet don't know how to achieve this, or let limiting beliefs paralyze progress and allow dreams to die. However, the principals and practices outlined in this book can apply to anyone reading it. It's time to let the excuses go. Our primary purpose is to revive your vision by breathing life into it and show you what you can achieve beyond your current circumstances so you can prosper.

This book is designed to touch on critical pain points, to feed you with knowledge and provide you with encouragement necessary to make forward movement and to challenge you to go beyond your comfort zone. Chances are, you are beyond contemplation and have already made a conscious decision to do something different with your life, which is why you have this book in your hand. Now that you are right at the edge, you just need the extra push so you can finally take that leap no matter how scary it may be. That is what we are here for.

First and foremost, let's get something crystal clear: you do not pick your purpose, it picks you, and that is the thing you must get passionate about. Second of all, we are not going to give you false hope by giving you some get rich quick scheme, as the connection between your passion and purpose is an emotional investment. Third, we are not anti-job or anti-education; in fact, we are proponents for both. However, a job should be utilized as an investor (i.e. a stakeholder who contributes financially toward your future without expectation of financial return), for job-specific skills (i.e. to accumulate the necessary experience) and as a stepping stone, as you make progress toward a much bigger goal. In other words, a job should be a temporary assignment that prepares you for the real work you are here to do and an education (traditional or non-traditional) is not a guarantee for a job. However, it does ensure a broader perspective on ways in which you can turn problems into opportunities when life challenges you. Educating yourself gives you a choice, which is our greatest power, and making a different choice will change the trajectory of your life in ways you may not have envisioned.

Trust and believe you do have what it takes to succeed, no matter what you have convinced yourself of up until now. Let us help you get rid of that bitter bite and find that irresistible sweet spot that brings a smile to your heart, just when thinking about doing what you love. Please be forewarned; we offer a hefty dose of truth and transparency in our discussions, no holds barred, so that we can deep dive into the heart of the matter and the underlying issues that have a tight grip on your life. It is likely that we will hit a nerve, as the truth does not necessarily feel good, but we like to keep our level of communication candid for the sake of your best interest. For that, we will not apologize. However, we do ask that you take a moment to pause and reflect on the hard truths as you relate to the information provided, fully acknowledging that taking risks feels vulnerable because it is uncertain and unpredictable, yet it is so liberating, proactive and healing. Most of all, it is a growth opportunity.

The biggest regret that any of us could ever have would be to have our story be the untold story. Please don't let that happen. The world needs you. Share your story with them. Now is your time to walk in your awesomeness.

CHAPTER 1: Invest in Yourself: You Owe it to You!

Understand your birthright.
You are entitled to live in your greatness!

"You don't have to be great to get started, but you have to get started to be great!" -Les Brown

Let's talk about making the connection of defining your passion and aligning it with your purpose so that you can walk in your awesomeness and breathe life into your vision. Do you believe you are worth the investment? We are here to tell you that you are worth the investment. To live the life you love beyond your wildest imagination, you have to recognize that you are entitled to the greatness that lives within you; that is unique to only you and you have to be willing to release your truths and share them with the world. Take a moment to embrace that. We are here to help you unleash the story inside of you so that you can passionately deliver the message the rest of the world needs to hear, with an understanding that it is your very story that will be powerful enough to transform someone else's life by letting them know they are not alone.

So, what makes you so special? Why are you entitled and what's so great about you? Simple answer: Your exposure to life. Life has prepared you for your arrival date. When you were born, you were given the gift of life, and the universe contributed to your life by branding you as an individual with undeniable talents, especially designed for you. Greatness comes in all sizes, shapes, and colors, which is what makes it so beautiful. It is only when distractions become the focus of your life rather than the less dominant factor in it that new motivation for how you will lead your life shows up. This pivotal understanding is the basis for every thought, every decision and every move you make thereafter.

When you are living your life on purpose and with meaning, you stop living your life depending on others to give you opportunities that you need to create for yourself. You are fully aware that you are in control of unlimited happiness. You set clear expectations for yourself and gain clarity about your intentions. You hold steadfast to your vision, and your commitment level never changes with circumstantial situations. You trust the process of life, knowing whatever energy you give to the universe will be returned (good, bad or indifferent). Entitled fulfillment is your birthright, which is your universal passport to travel abroad in life.

It's never too late: Walk in your awesomeness at any age!

Great news! Today is your lucky day! You no longer have to gamble your hard-earned money away, while waiting on the winning lottery numbers to foster your dreams. All bets are placed on you. You are the winning lottery ticket, and the only formula you need to guarantee your win are five key components: (1) a vision (2) your story (3) the passion (4) commitment and (5) faith. Nothing complex. In fact, it's so simple, you may have the tendency to make it too complicated.

Despite contrary belief, it is never too late to live the life you love. Everyone is deserving of a passion-filled life, but to walk in your awesomeness means you must begin with a change in mindset. Too often, we only dream and fantasize, or have an idea about the life we desire (our own business, the ideal relationship, good health, our dream home or car, to travel the world) and the reality is these dreams and fantasies will never come to fruition if you do not nurture them and practically fall in love with them and follow-up with a viable plan.

Once you have made up your mind, be determined, motivated and relentless about creating an abundant life for yourself no matter what! Envision your life today being the life you love. Describe it. What does it look like? What does it feel like? Where are you and who and what are you surrounded by? Next, assess your current situation by taking some time for yourself (wherever you can find it and without any excuses) and figure out what is working well for you and what is not working at all. Write these down on a notepad with blue or black ink and then take a red pen to draw a single line through the things you need to replace, change, or eliminate altogether. If it is not serving you well, it does not belong in your life.

Everyone has a unique gift. Define yours by digging deeper into the things that bring you joy. Ask yourself what is holding you back: what obstacles are in your way? Fear? Finances? Family obligations? A day-job? Limited time? Lack of a support system? Think about how you can create a different scenario. In other words, if it's fear, how can you overcome it? If it's finances, can you cut back on expenses or increase your income? If it's time, why not get up a little earlier, or stay up a little later to give yourself the time you need? Are those reality TV shows you allow to consume your life really worth it? Should you spend an excessive amount of time watching somebody else's life when you need to be improving your own? These are important factors in your life that must be considered in order for you to break free of a trapped situation. Finding a solution to these problems, in addition to your deliberate commitment, will open up limitless opportunities.

Your awesomeness may overwhelm you, but if you tell your truth to yourself every day about who you are and don't apologize for it, you will be empowered to concentrate on the bigger vision, so that you don't feel swallowed whole by the magnitude of you. Today is a day of celebration. We applaud you for having the courage and the appetite for something different. Now that you are here, acknowledge that you have moved the dot on the map. Knowing your desired destination and knowing how to get there from your present location puts you one step closer in the right direction. When in doubt, keep following the signs!

The system is broken, but you don't have to be.

Women, particularly women of color, have the tendency to deprive themselves of the better side of life. The universe is prepared to deliver everything we are entitled to, but we repeatedly talk ourselves out of accepting the good things that show up in our lives and choose the road of struggle instead. Many of us already come from broke and broken backgrounds, yet we eagerly buy into a broken system. Our parents teach us and society reinforces our learning, that we are to go to school and graduate, get a good job or land a great career opportunity, grow with the company and climb the corporate ladder, reap the benefits that come with working long-term for the same employer, retire well and live happily ever after.

The reality is that while that may sound like an ideal arrangement, the system repeatedly fails us and, by teaching our children the same, we are failing them. Schools do not teach financial literacy, they do not teach about entrepreneurship or business ownership, they do not teach anything about hitting the glass ceiling or what type of back-up plan to have. It does not prepare us for worst case scenarios (like losing a job and what to do if/when that happens). Although unemployment rates have returned to the typical pre-recession rates, (in fact, the current rate of 4.6% as of this writing makes it a record low since 2007), haven't you wondered why there are a multitude of job postings, but the challenges of landing that job interview have increased and getting hired is next to impossible?

The name of the game has changed. Gone are the days where you can walk into the office of any perspective employee, hand them your resume, land the interview and get hired. Nor can you pick-up the phone and call someone you know, request that they put in a good word for you and be given the opportunity to get your foot in the door. In today's job market and with advanced technology, you are at a bit of a disadvantage because it is mandatory for all applicants to apply for a job online. You must then meet the minimum qualifications listed on the job posting, which often includes a college degree in addition to required certifications and years of experience that you may lack in a particular specialty area. You are racing against time to get your application submitted because the recruiters receive such a high volume of incoming applications that companies must create a cut-off point. If you are applying for a job with a large company, hopefully your application has passed the screening process. Large corporations use a keyword-searchable database that scans resumes for words related to certain job vacancies, so if you do not use the most appropriate key words as it relates to the position you are interested in, you will surely be overlooked. This does not even include the grueling assessment test you will be challenged to pass before you will even be considered.

Now that you have done all of that, congratulations, you have just played the "hurry up to wait" game. The length of time it takes for a human being to contact you is absurd and when you call to check the status of your application, if you are fortunate enough to get a live person on the phone, you are told that they will contact you if interested. Once contacted, you need to prepare for a behavioral-based interview, which is an approach that looks at specific past behaviors to predict future performance. With an understanding that candidates cannot easily practice in advance and offer answers that the employers want to hear, this makes for a more unprompted and genuine interview than does a traditional interview. Depending on how you respond to the "tell me about a time when," "can you recall an instance where," and "describe a situation that" type questions, you may not be the chosen candidate. Meanwhile, your financial situation is deteriorating, you are under insurmountable stress and you are questioning your worth as it dwindles down to a minimum.

As if that isn't enough to frustrate you, if you happen to be one of the few lucky individuals selected for hire, it is very easy to become complacent. Although you may be able to make lateral moves within the organization, it becomes increasingly difficult to make vertical moves.

This may be due to limiting beliefs the woman holds about her abilities, or it may be due to the limitations the organization sets in exchange for an opportunity in an advanced role. Often, the demands placed on a female in a top leadership role, coupled with the female's responsibilities at home, create a greater burden on her and make accepting such a role less important. Perhaps you do climb the corporate ladder. The questions that remain are: how long does it truly take to get to the top? And once you've reached your destination, is that as far as you can go? Will you struggle to break through the glass ceiling in a male-dominated world? In some cases, where only a lateral move is possible, you may have to accept menial jobs where your talents are underutilized, just to keep a paycheck coming in, or you may have to work a second job for supplemental income just to make ends meet. Then there are those of you who are desperately seeking employment, so as not to further jeopardize your livelihood, but because you are overqualified, you are constantly being rejected since the employer cannot risk hiring you and utilize its resources to invest in someone who may not stay the course.

Let's suppose you do get offered the job. It is only an offer contingent upon the results of the on-boarding process. Meaning, you still need to receive clearance from Human Resources regarding your background check and from Employee Health regarding your physical exam, vaccinations and urine drug screening. If you have gotten this far, once hired, you will need to attend new hire orientation to learn about the company, get acclimated to your new position, new systems, company policies and procedures (which may not be clearly defined) and the culture of the organization, all while continuing to make the best impression possible. If you have demonstrated your abilities to the employer's expectations, you can move past the 90-day probationary period and become a permanent employee. Keep in mind that most states have adopted the employment 'at-will' law, which means an employee can be fired at any time, for any reason, without good cause. There are few legal categories that protect the employee against discrimination, harassment and retaliation; your legal rights for fighting termination are very limited.

Now that you have gone through that painful process, as time passes, you find yourself entrenched in the complex organizational hierarchies that are linked to the bureaucracies of Corporate America: office politics, rigid conformity to formal practices, the excessive red tape that binds the employee and prevents forward movement and upper management making final decisions without input from front line staff. Let's not forget that within the 8, 10 or 12 hours shifts you signed up for, while you are exhausting yourself for a job that has you living paycheck to paycheck, being micromanaged, under the direction of poor leadership and lacking the freedom, flexibility and control, you are surrounded by employees who bring nothing but negative energy into your space, as they gossip, protest, complain and criticize all that is not working well and in their favor. Yet, they have no intention of doing anything about it, all of which declines workplace morale and has one questioning: Why am I here? You try to leave work separate from your home life, but that can be difficult to do for some, especially if you have no outlet. Before you know it, you have allowed yourself to be consumed by your job and you take your work issues home, leaving little time or energy for your family or yourself. You go back the next day and do it all over again. It is a maddening cycle.

Workers need jobs; employers need workers, but the job market is uncertain and the so-called "recession-proof" careers we once thought existed are no more. You may very well, as many have, find yourself unexpectedly laid off and unemployed, which may quickly and drastically turn your life upside down. It's all a game and, unfortunately, you need to know how to play it just right, or you lose.

Jobs are plentiful. However, educated women sometimes lack the skill-set that match the business needs of the perspective employers. A higher education plus experience is required for many entry-level positions, which discourages job seekers who do not meet the minimum qualifications. Those who decide to obtain a higher education end up with low paying jobs, possibly in the unemployment line, putting them in unnecessary debt. Employers are hesitant to hire new graduates because they either have no capacity to train, or no budget to create training programs for the high volume of candidates banging the doors to get in. These are just a few of the reasons women are moving away from traditional work and stressful roles, towards more satisfying roles in the world of business. These are also the reasons that make it so imperative to teach women how to become economically self-sufficient and less dependent on a society that keeps us ill-prepared for economic downturn. Not only do we need to learn how to create opportunities for ourselves, but to create jobs for others by building businesses throughout our communities.

Women are looking for flexibility, fulfillment and a true work/life balance for sustained gratification, and they are not finding this within the organizations they are employed by. Instead, they end up with a J.O.B., which keeps them "Just Over Broke," broken emotionally and seemingly trapped in a broken system. The truth is the system that we entangle ourselves in robs us of our time, our energy and our freedom. But, the biggest thief of them all is US because we do not allow ourselves another way out. Instead, we stay committed to locking ourselves in and blaming everyone but ourselves for the predicaments we create.

No system or person or group of individuals should have that much power over your life. It should not be left to your employer to control your destiny. Entrepreneurship is the new movement, ladies! Women want a piece of the business ownership pie and they are no longer asking for permission, they are making announcements and demanding that you step aside if you have no plans to join the movement.

Know your worth and determine your destiny.

BREAKING NEWS: We interrupt this program to make an important announcement! You are not for sale. You are the rightful owner of you and the talents you were gifted with by your creator. You may choose to rent your services from time to time, or perhaps you have interest in donating your gifts to those who would benefit from them. However, neither scenario comes with a price tag. You are invaluable and an amazing asset to this world and the people who need you the most have been searching for you, hoping, praying and waiting for you to show up. They need to feel your presence, hear your words of wisdom and find strength in your encouragement. But most of all, they need to heal through your story, through the powerful message you need to deliver to them. It is you and only you who has your unique ability and you are the one who has been chosen to contribute and serve humanity by sharing your gift.

Poverty is one of several terms used in the American Financial Class System (AFCC) by which the U.S. Census Bureau uses to describe the income category your household falls under. However, you do not have to be categorized, because poverty is a state of mind more than it is a financial class. No matter what your current financial situation is, your mindset does not have to match it. You can be considered poor per the guidelines of the AFCC, but adopt a rich mindset. A rich mindset would consist of a different choice of words. For example, rather than saying you are poor or broke, you would say you are financially challenged, or you are experiencing a temporary set-back. In other words, your psychological relationship with money and your belief system surrounding success don't make you devoted to it; it means that you need to change your relationship with it and your mentality about it. Doing so would mean the difference between knowing your worth and de-valuing your ability to achieve something more.

Knowing your worth means that you are fully aware that you are priceless and the value you hold is immeasurable. It means that investing in yourself is non-negotiable. It means that you firmly believe in your capabilities and you are solid in knowing what you have to offer. It means that you don't work for free, you can't be bought and you are not a willing participant of the modern-day slave trade. It comes with an understanding that stepping out in faith doesn't cost a thing, and yet, if you don't ever take a step forward and push past limiting beliefs, it can cost you everything. Knowing your worth means that you will stop asking for handouts, looking for someone to give you a pass or allowing another entity to rob you of your prosperity. Knowing your worth means that you and many before you have already paid your dues. It means that you are certain you are here to contribute to something greater than yourself and that your life mission is your biggest prized possession and you will stop at nothing to win it.

Can you imagine what it would be like to have someone hand you an agenda or an itinerary with a plan and clear instructions for you to follow every single day of your life? How about being driven in a direction opposite of what you requested, or to a destination you didn't ask to be at? Would you just sit back, relax and enjoy the ride? How long would this go on before you decided to take the wheel and create and adhere to your own agenda? What would it take to convince you that your life should not be controlled by anyone other than you and your creator? In fact, this is a partnership and you are the co-creator, the Chief Executive Officer (CEO) of your life, just as every industry has a CEO to control business operations. A CEO has the most coveted title, but with that comes the most critical role: she is ultimately responsible for the success or failure of the company. The CEO sets the strategy and direction based on the vision of the organization; that is the primary responsibility, just as it should be your primary responsibility to have a vision for your life, create and execute a plan and follow the directions on your roadmap as you evolve.

Does this sound like tremendous pressure and a lot of work? Of course, it is. No one said it is an easy road to take. Otherwise, this book and many others would not be necessary to write because everyone would take that route, no questions asked. But, is it worth it? Yes, it absolutely is. It always feels better to do the work required to reach your goals than it does to do nothing at all, while you hope, wish and fantasize about a better outcome.

Growing up, my (Catrina's) mother would always say, "Opportunity never knocked on anybody's door, so if you want opportunity, you have to go out there and look for it."

Opportunity is everywhere. That's what's so exciting! You don't have to look very far, or for very long, but you do have to look for it or create it. If you are going to get to your destiny, you must stay determined and if you want to determine your destiny, you must remain in the CEO position. It is your prerogative to hire a team for help and delegate some responsibilities; you may even prefer to consult with some of those team members. Just remember, it is ultimately your responsibility to control your life, your vision and your happiness.

CHAPTER 2: Who Are You Meant to Be? Reveal Your Authentic Self

Self-discovery: Confidently stand in your truth.

"The only person you are destined to become is the person you decide to be." -Ralph Waldo Emerson

Peel back the layers and get to the core of who you are. We wear many faces, many hats and many layers; but, at the deepest core of your being lays the truth of who you are. When you pretend to be somebody you are not and choose to hide behind a disguise, you can easily get lost living in second-hand experiences. First-hand experiences come only when you choose to be your authentic self and when you are true to who you are and are willing to confidently stand in your truth. That is when true fulfillment rises to the occasion to celebrate the real you.

In this lifetime, you deserve to know who you are and why you are, so that you can gain a deeper level awareness, expand your understanding, identify with what, when and how you can best serve and connect with others who will benefit the most from your truth. Your awareness will effortlessly do the work for you when your true self shows up because your principal purpose in life is to evolve every day. When we can connect with ourselves, we will easily connect with others. You will only develop such a connection by going through a self-discovery process.

STEP 1:

Belief is the first step in this process. The belief you hold about yourself will either greatly enhance your life or greatly diminish it. Your beliefs may be obvious, or they can be buried in the subconscious mind. Either way, whatever they are, however noticeable or hidden, your thoughts and spoken words bring power to their existence and it is how you see yourself in this world. So, it is imperative that you examine your beliefs and form a healthier identity of you.

STEP 2:

Ask and Listen is the second step in this process. Ask yourself "Who am I?" and follow it with "I am ____" (you fill in the blank). Create a list of "I AMs" and pay attention to what words follow. This ties into your belief system, but as you gain clarity with what you believe about yourself, in Step 2, you will be in a better position to list positive words that follow "I AM," rather than negative words. Speaking aloud and repetitive writing reinforces our learning, so this would be a good time to bring those hidden negative beliefs to the forefront and challenge yourself by replacing those beliefs with positive words that are visible and accessible to you.

STEP 3:

Trust is the third step in this process. You have to trust the truth of what you have discovered about yourself and be willing to accept it for what it is. This is the step that enables you to repair what is broken, replace it with something better, or remove it if it has no potential. This step in the process is the renewal phase. It allows you to shed excess weight, open your life up to unlimited possibilities and restores your faith to know that hard work and dedication equal results. Therefore, you can change your perception and your expectations.

BELIEVE. ASK. RECEIVE.

Life experiences shape our stories and lead our journey.

Life experiences are our greatest lessons if we are paying attention to the details of our lives. If we are paying attention, we will notice that there is a succession of life lessons and if you live through them, you have a better understanding of what they mean and what purpose they serve. You will also have a greater appreciation for free education; although, not learning your lesson does come with a price. You cannot escape life without growing pains and mistakes. These are valuable because they show us what areas of our lives we are flawed in and give us the opportunity to approach the situation differently when it shows up again so we can improve upon it. By the way, it will show up again and again until you've learned the lesson, not necessarily as the same presentation, but in a recognizable format. Once you own the victory, you move on to the next lesson, or several lessons simultaneously, which means you are an experienced player. Therefore, you advance to the next level.

These lessons, be them about love, joy, success or liberation, inevitably come with heartache, regret, failure and pain. These must correspond in this manner because it's what gives shape to our stories. It is necessary to have pain in our life lessons because pain gives us pause. Pause is that silent gap of time we need to catch our breath and to be still in the moment, so we can feel what is taking place rather than just go through the motions. These emotions teach us coping mechanisms and survival skills; they are motivators that compel us to take action, and they influence us to make better decisions. For example, if we experienced love in a romantic relationship without experiencing heartache, perhaps the depth of our vulnerability and risk-taking skills would not have been fully challenged. If we experienced a life of joy and never had any regrets, perhaps lacking a deeper connection for creating change or growing into an empathetic individual would have made us none the wiser. If we succeeded in every aspect of our life and never experienced failure, there would be no protective layer to shield us from injuries, our egos would get in the way and we wouldn't be humbled. If we experienced liberation without having ever experienced the pain of confinement, perhaps we would not know a greater value of ourselves to push past fear.

The choices we make are the driving force behind the path we take. Based on our present predicament, we make the decision we feel is best for our situation. However, many times we make poor decisions, or we let our situations play out, and they don't work in our favor. When this happens, we may choose to make a different decision, or to do nothing more. In either case, your life will play out according to the decisions you've made. Our stories are then developed from that path from which the life experiences we are challenged with determine our next steps. In this way, stories lead our journey. As an essential human need, we crave an understanding about life in general and have a need to know specifically how and where we fit into this universe. Some of us search for the answer all of our lives and never find it. As your own story unfolds right in front of you, you have to pay attention to the details and gather the clues that will help you put together the meaning of your life. We live in such a hurried environment these days, but sometimes we have to pause for the cause and get clear about what our life is telling us.

The patterns of your life that repeatedly show up are powerful because they are the biggest clues to capture the essence of your story. These patterns should evoke emotions that inspire and motivate you to make a difference in your life and the lives of others. Think about it for a moment: how much time do you spend watching your favorite reality TV shows, or a movie on Netflix, cable, RedBox or in theaters? What about the books we read, or the plays we attend, or the songs we play and sing to, or the stories we share in social settings with family, friends or colleagues, the news we tune into, or the internet we consistently surf? We are completely immersed in story-telling. Telling stories is a great way to communicate. They allow us to speculate and make our own judgments, to connect with one another, explore endless possibilities and find solutions to our problems. So why not take the time to reflect on and dissect your own story and change your outcome by changing your story? Can you imagine what your life would look like if you put more time into understanding your personal story rather than solely focusing on everyone else's? Amazing results will come from this. Plant yourself in the best version of your story, nourish it daily and watch it grow!

CHOICE is our greatest power. Make a different choice.

We have no purpose without choice. Choice is engrained in everything we do, and it gives us direction, independence, and power to create our experiences. You are in control of your own life through the choices you make. External forces, such as the economy, the environment or people, may very well influence some of your choices and your final decision will be made based on how flexible or rigid your choices are and what factors are involved, but the choice is still yours to make. You may choose to wear pink instead of purple, commute a different route to work, choose not to eat breakfast or not wear make-up today. These are the kind of choices that are simple choices to make because they don't require much thought and they are flexible. Some choices are more rigid; you have a certain deadline to meet, or a particular schedule you must adhere to, such as work or school. However, you could also choose not to adhere to these restrictive choices and deal with the consequences. You can choose to change your mind about your previous choice. You can get up every day and choose to do nothing at all, or you can choose to do as much as you can possibly fit into one day. You may choose to keep doing the same ol' thing you've been doing for years, or you can choose to do something different. The choice is up to you.

What we can tell you for sure is that your life is only on hold for as long as you choose to put it on hold. You are only one choice away from making a significant difference in your life. You can stand still in a moment, but standing still for a lifetime is painful. Have you taken the time to evaluate your life and see with your own two eyes that years have passed and you are no better off today than you were all those years ago? Why would it make sense to stay in a position of no movement at all, or one that creates backward movement instead of forward movement? Reality check! You cannot choose both directions. You either choose to go backward or you choose to go forward. You've already played it safe...too safe, and where has that gotten you? Life naturally offers some level of risk and, admittedly, taking a risk can feel very frightening. We get it. However, there is no risk in stagnancy or decisions that cause your life to regress.

There is nothing wrong with calculated risks; it is perfectly fine that you gauge the distance of your jump so you have some idea of where you might land. Each time you prepare for your jump, you challenge yourself to go a little bit further. The idea is to gain the momentum necessary to make the jump, regardless of the distance, and realize that your calculations may be a little bit off. We know the million and one excuses we all make to stay within our comfort zones but, at some point, we must get out of our comfort zones and challenge ourselves to be more, do more and have more. Let go of those warm blanket of excuses we love to stay wrapped up in for as long as we can and make a different choice today.

Get passionate about the message inside of you.

"There is no greater agony than bearing an untold story inside of you." -Maya Angelou

What message are you holding on to that you have not yet shared with anyone? What story is brewing inside of you? These are the questions we once asked ourselves before we realized how agonizing it was to keep our stories a secret and take them to our graves. What help does this offer and what difference does it make? The one question that was once posed to an audience we happened to be a part of, which especially resonated with us, is this: What signifies the most important part of your life, your date of birth or your date of death? The audience pondered over this questioned and yelled out one or the other, but surprisingly the answer was the dash between these dates.

The dash symbolizes our entire lives from the day we were born until the day we die. What will be said about you in your eulogy? What significant contributions did you make in life? You see, the dash represents all the years you spent living on earth. But, it's what you've done with your life in all those years that establishes your dash's worth.

There is a beautifully written poem by Linda Ellis called "The Dash, " and we'd like to share it with you in case you haven't yet heard it. We hope you enjoy it.

For it matters not, how much we own, the cars, the house, the cash,
What matters is how we live and love and how we spend our dash.
So, think about this long and hard; Are there things you would like to change?
For you never know how much time is left that can still be rearranged.
If we could just slow down enough to consider what is true and real
and always try to understand the way other people feel.
And be less quick to anger and show appreciation more
and love the people in our lives like we have never loved before.
If we treat each other with respect and more often wear a smile,

Remembering that this special dash might only last a little while.

So, when your eulogy is being read with your life's actions to rehash…

Would you be proud of the things they say about how you spent your dash?

Be seen. Be heard. Be you: Share your vision, share your story.

No matter how different we'd like to think we are, we are more alike than we'd like to admit. Every individual has the same basic needs: the need for food, water, clothing, shelter, and safety. We also have a need to be validated. We all want to know if we matter. Beyond our troubling past and the history we hold, outside of our appearance and everything superficial, without judgment and harsh criticism, do I matter? We want to be seen, to be heard and to be our true selves. So, how do we get there? What does that mean for us individually? It means that, without a shadow of a doubt, we are here to love, be loved, teach, learn and prosper. We do this by sharing our vision and sharing our stories because "words are powerful. Put into action, they are life changing" (Carol L. Rickard).

Words have a deep impact on us. Words can build us up or break us down. Words can hurt us or help us. Words can embrace our desire to live our best life or allow us to settle for mediocrity. Words can be put to a melodic tune and set our moods to feel happy, sad, disappointed, lonely, heart-broken, loved, empty, full, inspired, encouraged and numerous other emotions.

Words mold us from a very early age. Just let that settle for a minute. When you were little, the words of your mother and father helped you identify who you are, where you come from, why you're here, what you want to be when you grow up and when it's time to put your belief system (based on your morals and values) in effect. You rely on the words that surrounded you growing up. Words allow us the opportunity to prosper, to get stronger, to satisfy basic human needs, to feel a sense of belonging, to connect with others, to challenge one another, to express ourselves and to conquer some things we otherwise could not.

On the other hand, words can be demeaning, disrespectful, harmful, destructive, unfair, cold and calloused, lifeless and out of control. Words can make us feel at our lowest and hinder our ability to change or make light of a dark situation. Of course, these are the type of words that don't allow us to reach our highest potential and these are the type of words we hear too frequently in our culture today (in our music, on TV, in our children's schools, on the streets and in our homes). There are little to no consequences for those who are responsible for speaking them, but heavy consequences on those who hear them. As you share your story, it will resonate with other people. It will help them also see and have it seem more achievable and believable. Inside, we are all wired for success. But now is your time for action. Now is the time to begin taking incremental steps toward your goal. We're not talking about something that's an overnight success, but simply emotionally investing and putting in the hard work. You have to take action.

That said, understanding the power you hold in your ability to share your story is not only beautiful, but it is a responsible thing to do. Stories are meant to be shared. It would be hard to imagine a life without shared stories and shared visions. The world would be bleak, and our souls would be hugely deficient. So, get excited about your story and be willing to share it with the world! If there was just one life you could change based on your story alone, wouldn't that be worth it?

CHAPTER 3: Define and Align, Connecting Passion and Purpose.

Get connected (mind, body, and soul): Meditation and prayer.

Get still to get connected. Quiet your mind, deactivate your body from being in motion and relax your soul. Because we live in a fast-paced, forward-moving environment, we have become a society that is uncomfortable being in silence. It is not natural for all of us; even silence is not so silent in the minds of most. Sometimes it seems much easier to keep the body still, but the mind can be challenging to control because we have so many thoughts that constantly come up. That is why we have to practice meditation, to heighten our concentration and to bring a deeper level of awareness into our space along with peace and calmness that is only felt and understood by your inner being. Teaching your mind to concentrate on one thing at a time in the midst of the chaos that lives within our minds, or surrounds us on the outside, is initially difficult to master, but with time, you will.

Mantras, which are sacred words that are repeated, offer the cluttered mind a mental release to let go and let flow because it gives you a narrow focus. Same is true if you narrowed your focus to a single object, like a candlelight, or a single thought. So, while we live in a noisy external world, we can learn to create a world without noise within ourselves. What a concept.

By learning this beneficial practice, you are creating peace from the inside out, experiencing a oneness with the self and the universe and getting to the truth of who you are and why you exist, at the depth of your core. It is here that tranquility finds its way to truth and transparency, and clarity shows up. This is a spiritual experience, and it is a powerful meeting of the mind.

Prayer is more religious-based. So depending on your faith, you would be praying to the highest, most divine power known to mankind, whether you call this divine power God, Allah, Jehovah, Jah, Lord, Heavenly Father, The Almighty, Master, or whatever name you give our creator, the relationship you establish with him on a more intimate basis, is your right. You know your prayers, and He knows your heart.

We happen to call him God and, without imposing our beliefs on you, we find that when we go to him and tell him what we need, while continuing to stay in action and remain patient, on his time, he does answer and he does provide. When you are still and embrace his very existence, he showers you with heavy blessings. The secret to staying blessed is to get "an attitude of gratitude." Before you can receive more of what you want, you have to be thankful for what you have. So, your job is to come up with a least five new things (every single morning) that you are grateful for. The truth may be that you wake up with aches and pains, don't have a job, have a bucket on wheels for a car, can hardly provide for your kids and live in a tiny apartment that doesn't have more than the basic features.

You, or the next person, who is dealt the same hand, can find the blessings in every complaint. For instance, your blessings would sound something like this: Thank you God for blessing me with all of my senses and all of my limbs, I may be in pain, but at least I can still move; thank you God for waking me up this morning, for giving me the opportunity to do today what I did not do yesterday; thank you

God for my car, it may not be much, but it's transportation that gets me from point A, to point B, and it's fully paid for; thank you God for my tiny apartment, it lacks in space and fancy amenities, but it provides a roof over our heads and a safe place for me and my children and one day, my hard work will pay off and afford us something better; thank you God for my health, my strength and for a loving and supportive family. You see? Same scenarios, but different perspectives.

In combination, prayer and meditation are powerful tools, and both are worth engaging in, as these are life-changing experiences. But remember, you can't just depend on making it on a wing and a prayer, you have to keep moving toward whatever it is you are trying to achieve.

Self-assessment: Look within. Reflect on what continues to show up.

Have you ever truly paid close attention to the things that continue to show up in your life? Perhaps it showed up in the numerous personality tests you've taken, or maybe it was in your conversations with others. Could it have appeared in the articles or books you've read or the seminars you attend? What is the thing you are most attracted to, the one thing that brings you so much joy just thinking about it? What is the talent you have that you are most passionate about and what is that one hobby you absolutely cannot do without, that if taken away from you, would make you feel empty? What comes naturally for you and what is the thing that, no matter how much you try to ignore it, it keeps pulling on your heart strings with urgency to get your undivided attention? What is that thing that gives you so much gratification, you would do it for free?

These are the types of questions you must ask yourself as a part of your self-assessment. These are the questions that will get you closer to your answer. The process of reflecting means that you are holding a mirror up to yourself.

Let's go through a brief exercise. We call this the "Engagement Party" because it is a process by which you are looking past your current situation and making a solid commitment to the new you. So go to the mirror and stand in front of it and please note: Negative self-talk is not invited to this engagement party!

The first thing we want you to do is to give yourself a great, big hug and congratulate yourself for your willingness to make a new commitment to you! Now, hold your hands out, with your palms in an upright and open position, as if someone is going to give you something. Next, you will engage in positive self-talk gazing in your eyes, as you look in the mirror in front of you and repeat the following:

'Hello, beautiful. I am so honored to be invited to such an awe-mazing engagement party today. I, (fill in the blank with your first, middle and last name), do solemnly promise as I stand before you on (date), to become the best version of myself that I can possibly be and live the best life I can possibly live.

I know what my life looks like today and although I cannot change the environment around me, I can and I will change any limiting beliefs I hold about myself and I will challenge myself to do more and more each day as I reach toward my goals.

Today, I hold a vision for myself that is absolutely achievable and, as long as I stay in action and have a positive outlook, I will get there. I am grateful for all that I have now, and I will remain grateful as I continue to be blessed.

Thank you for believing in me, thank you for trusting me and thank you for reminding me what a gift I am to this world. Today, I choose to walk in my awe-someness because I refuse to live with my regrets or die with my dreams. Today, I choose YOU because you are worth the investment!'

Now sign and date this commitment and put it on your mirror, so you can review it every day and adhere to it.

A vision board is also a powerful visualization tool. It is a collage of images, words, quotes, prayer passages, personal mantras, etc., creatively arranged on a poster board, that serves to continually remind you of your passion and purpose. It is a wonderful way to display the bigger dream or vision you have for yourself and channel your positive energy to it. The rationale behind a vision board is to demonstrate how you view your future life and then speak it into existence. So that it is not "out of sight, out of mind," you will want to place this in an area that you will see it daily. You may also choose, if you wish, to meditate and/or pray over it, as this would be one of a few ways you can breathe life into your vision.

Here is a list of materials (at minimum) you will need. Please feel free to add variation:

- A poster board, cork board or canvas (24x24 or larger)

- Pins, tape, thumbtacks, or glue (Rubber Cement works well for cut and paste projects)

- Scissors, markers, paint

- Magazines (old magazines you have at home, or FREE magazines at the library)

- A picture of yourself in the middle of the board (optional)

The Process:

This project will take some time. It is not something you would want to rush through, so set aside some "me time" (approximately 3 hours is recommended - it could take more or less time) and set-up a therapeutic environment (e.g. candles and music that inspire you sets the mood nicely). This can be a very freeing experience, so take advantage of it.

NOTE: You should be able to find most of the images, words, etc., in the magazines. However, if for any reason you can't find what you need, there is always the internet.

Now that you have the materials you need and are in a quiet, uninterrupted space, you are prepared to create your vision board!

STEP 1:

Close your eyes and take three deep breaths. What do you envision your ideal life to look like? Give this some thought and take your time as you ponder over your ideas.

STEP 2:

If you choose, place a photo of yourself in the center of your board and work around this image. If you don't choose, place whatever image here that you find most meaningful. Either way, you will be working from the center outward.

STEP 3:

Cut out images that represent the life you desire. We find the easiest way to determine this is to think about each aspect of your new abundant life and categorize it. For example, in your new abundant life, there are four main categories, or aspects of your life: (A) Relationships (B) Health (C) Spirituality and (D) Wealth - not necessarily in this order.

STEP 4:

The images, words, quotes and such should speak to your thoughts and emotions as it relates to the categories listed in step 3. So, it should look and feel tangible; it should bring you good vibes when you are in its presence, and it should keep you balanced, in harmony, at peace and focused on your goals. These are the images and words you want to cut out.

STEP 5:

Before you adhere your images and words to the board, take a moment to arrange (and rearrange as necessary) these items, to ensure they are exactly where you'd like them on the board. Don't get too hung up on this step; you can make this step very simple by sorting what you have cut out and arrange them accordingly.

That's it! You've got yourself a vision board. Frame it if you want, place it in plain view, take action every day and watch your life change as you stay committed to change.

Mindset shift: You don't need permission to live the life you were meant to live.

To a great extent, we have been told most, if not all of our lives, what life is supposed to look like. If we are fortunate enough to have caring individuals in our lives that have good intentions for us, they should offer us guidance and provide us with support. We are given precise instructions on how to create a life for ourselves that, although practical, is governed by society's standards. We get caught up in the cobwebs of this belief system, and we forget to dream bigger for ourselves. Instead, we get settled in boundaries.

This broken system is set up to serve us for a short period of time. Eventually, we outgrow it; we become too big to fit into the ideals we have been prepared for. So, we must create a paradigm shift within our mindset. We do this by disconnecting from the old system and dialing into a new system. As we said earlier, if something no longer serves us well, we must let it go because it has no place in our lives.

Just as an old phone number is disconnected, you would typically get an auto-recording that states, "We're sorry, you have reached a line that is either disconnected or no longer in service," a new phone number is then reprogrammed and rerouted to take its place so that you can be reached. Similarly, when your mind is disconnected or desensitized from the old belief system, the new mindset must be reprogrammed and rerouted so new information can reach you. When you dial into the new system (i.e. new way of thinking), the notification will state, "We appreciate your call, and we're glad you have chosen to connect to the newly downloaded system."

We need to go on a journey of self-discovery to really know who we are and what we're meant to do. We must embrace our purpose. We must allow the passion that we have for our greatness to spark. It's time to let go of that negative self-talk. It's time to begin living our life working for something more. There's a secret to making that happen: it's learning to be grateful for what you have already. This is huge. Embracing all that you do have in your life is one of the greatest ways that you can begin to see a possibility of abundance, rather than focusing on the scarcity. Your belief will show you the path to move from the belief that you're living in scarcity to the reality that you were always meant to live in abundance.

The truth is, you do not need permission to live the life you were meant to live, but you aren't able to openly receive inspiration, or gain access to new information, nor can you properly be influenced to change your circumstances and have a positive outlook on life, unless and until you allow yourself to be released from the burden of the old mentality and then infused with a new school of thought. Then and only then, can the mind-shift occur.

How to get unstuck: Start from where you are and work with what you have.

Each and every one of us is as unique as our DNA, our fingerprint, and our social security number. There are no two people who are completely identical to one another, down to every fiber of their being. Let that simmer a moment, because that is absolutely a divine phenomenon.

No two people are alike. So, this would mean there is no other person in this great, big world, who can do what you do in the way that you do it. It may seem like every innovative idea has already been thought of, but it simply isn't true. In reality, there is so much of the American Dream to be shared that there is a large slice that has been carved out and saved especially for you. It has your name on it. So how do you get unstuck? How do we stop feeling so over-whelmed with fear that we become disabled? What does it take to get from point A to point B without feeling lost in an unfamiliar environment? The answer is: Start from where you are, work with what you have and plant one foot in front of the next.

When you walk into a large mall, particularly one that you had never visited before and realize how massive the establishment is, doesn't an overwhelming feeling come over you? Do you decide to leave this unfamiliar, enormous mall and go to a more familiar, smaller mall? Or do you stay and feel your way around the new environment? More than likely, you choose the latter of the two. The first thing you do is look for the mall's directory and map and find out where you are. Once you have identified the bright red "You Are Here" symbol, you immediately begin to search the directory for your destination areas and the landmarks surrounding them; then you maneuver your way around until you get there. If you should get a little lost or confused on the way, there are signs you can depend on, a centralized information booth and many people in the mall from shoppers to employees for you to ask questions and be pointed in the right direction.

The point is, you may feel alone and like you don't have the resources you need when you are first getting started, but there is plenty of help available to you. When you are ready, truly, truly ready to start your business, no matter how overwhelming it may seem, when you start to seek out help to guide you on your journey, you will find it. There are people who can help you with the planning aspects of your business. There are people who can tell you what financial assistance is available to you, there are mentors who are eager to work with you, there are professional associations, local chamber of commerce offices and business development professionals that can provide you with guidance. There are a plethora of seminars, webinars and social events that offer networking opportunities where you can meet and surround yourselves with positive energy and like-minded individuals who are willing to help.

There is one minor caveat to all of this, and that is you have to make the first move if you ever want people to know you exist. Everyone has to start somewhere, but just get started. Social media venues are a great way to establish your presence in the business world. In fact, it is no longer an option to use social media; it is expected for anyone who wants to be taken seriously. There are multitudes of platforms you could utilize and amongst them are Twitter, LinkedIn, Facebook, Instagram, Pinterest,

YouTube, Yelp and so much more. These are considered essential to the success of any business. The best part is that these are user-friendly sites, so they are very easy to set-up, even for technically challenged people. Plus, they don't require much of your time or energy and can be fun to create. This is the best way to promote your brand in the marketplace and they are free!

There is no time like the present to get started, so don't procrastinate. Jump on this incredible opportunity by marking today as your "You Are Here" starting point and keep moving toward your goals every day until you have reached your final destination!

Freedom + Power + Fulfillment = A True Success Story.

Free yourself by creating the life you love! Your success story starts with your message, adds to your passion and ends with your legacy. What do you want to be remembered for? That is the question we need to focus your attention on. You determine this by discovering what matters to you most, identifying your values, thinking about whose lives you want to touch, what contributions you want to make in your community and what mark you want to leave in this world long after you're gone. Words are the catalyst for change, just as they are the building blocks of your legacy. So, in what ways can you use your words to empower others? In uncertain times, where so much negative energy surrounds people, what can you do to lift their spirits? With an understanding that you don't have to be an iconic figure to make a difference in someone's life, how can you contribute to society and stamp your fingerprint on your life's work as your milestones have been achieved?

What is your greatest power? We all have one. Tap into that power within you, and you will achieve great things in this lifetime. Do you love to teach? Do you have a special place in your heart for individuals with special needs? Are you a nurturer by nature? Do you like solving problems? Are you good at creating things? Are you talented at writing? Do you have a gift at storytelling or influencing large groups of people? What is it in you that you can give of yourself for the benefit of someone else?

For example, we absolutely love to help people in many ways, especially youth and women. It is our passion to educate, we are talented in speaking and writing, and we are creative thinkers. Working with those in underserved communities is close to our heart, and we care about worldwide societal issues surrounding health and wellness, equality issues that specifically target the African-American and LGBT communities and a variety of women's issues. So, we place our concentration on these areas and give back by contributing our time, energy and money. We volunteer, donate money to charitable organizations that help women and children in need and as business owners, we provide guidance and support through mentorship for aspiring female entrepreneurs. We also pay it forward for those who helped us along the way by performing random acts of kindness.

As you can see, we have found fulfillment in satisfying our craving to help others, by combining our talents with our passion and finding opportunities to give without expecting anything in return. It's about using your gifts to serve others in this world for the betterment of humanity. So again we ask: what do you want to be remembered for? What will your legacy be? When you can answer this question, and you start to participate in your life's mission, you will know you are living in your purpose because there will be no other feeling like it and it will be a true success story. Freedom. Power. Fulfillment.

CHAPTER 4: Build Your Business CORE: Exercise Daily to Increase Stamina

Warm-up: Leverage the power of a changed mind.

Welcome to our "Re-Boot Camp Academy™." We are your personal business mentors, but you can think of us as your personal fitness trainers because, similarly, we will be exercising your mind rather than your body. Same concept, different strategy. Just as a personal fitness trainer would be helping you re-condition your body, re-shape your physical appearance and increase stamina, we will be reconditioning your mind, re-shaping your beliefs about success and increasing your resilience. Core muscles in your body include the muscles in your pelvis, lower back, hips, and abdomen. Your core muscles in business include a specific set of skills: leadership, strategic planning, operations management, sales and marketing, customer service and communication, accounting/finance and Human Resources (AKA people management). Of course, there are other muscles in the body and in business that will support your growth and momentum, but building your business core is necessary. Your core is the strongest set of complex muscles that sustains a healthy body, and so will be the CORE of your business muscles used to sustain a healthy business.

As with any exercise, before we begin, we must start with a warm-up. The purpose of doing warm-up exercises is to gradually warm-up your muscles and allow them to be more flexible. This helps you be more efficient, lessens the risk of injury and improves your overall performance. Starting a business is certainly a painstaking process, but you don't have to be in unnecessary pain or prolong the soreness in the process.

Let's start with a brief warm-up session that will only take about five or ten minutes:

First: Sit in a comfortable, quiet place and close your eyes. Now, take in 3-5 slow, deep breaths. Get into the habit of doing this because there will be moments throughout the day when you will need to practice this in order to bring calmness into your space.

Second: Invite some positive words of encouragement into your day. REPEAT the following with as much enthusiasm as you can give:

- [ ] Today is going to be an exceptionally great day!

- [ ] No matter what happens today, I am going to keep an optimistic attitude!

- [ ] For every negative thought, I will come up with three positive thoughts!

- [ ] My word is only as good as my action!

- [ ] I am grateful for all that I have and for having the courage to do something different!

Third: Envision your day by creating a mental picture of it (as many details as possible – who, what, when, where and how). Now remind yourself why you do what you do and smile for being the chosen one.

Run at your own pace: Exercise your rights!

Now it's time to move! You may run at your own pace, but you must keep moving! The only exception to this rule is to take a brief pause when necessary to breathe and collect your thoughts. Try to keep this to a minimum, no more than 3-5 minute intermittent breaks. This is very important because when we slow down for longer than that, we lose momentum and we need momentum to keep going. It will be a bit challenging at first, but we don't expect you to be proficient in running a marathon right out of the gate. However, we do expect that you are capable enough to walk fast or jog. As you practice daily, you will gain more energy and naturally be able to do more, but please feel free at any time, to gently push yourself to go somewhat beyond your comfort level to maximize your exercise experience.

On a slightly deeper level, we need to get you emotionally invested in your business concept. You practically have to fall in love with your idea, and that starts with developing a relationship and nurturing it. You will need to be your biggest fan and loudest cheerleader, especially when times are tough. Otherwise, it's too easy to allow your dreams to be drowned out by the sound of fear and doubt. Fear and doubt dishonor how great you truly are, so stay true to you.

Are you ready and excited to move on to the next stages of exercise? So are we, but first. . .

Let us read you your rights!

- You have the right to be entitled to owning your life!

- You have the right to be fulfilled by doing the things that make you the happiest!

- You have the right to feel great about the talents you possess!

- You have the right to dream big and live even bigger than your imagination!

- You have the right to choose exactly where you want to be in life!

- You have the right to discover your authentic self and create your own successes!

You also have the right to remain silent, be still and do nothing, but how has that served you so far? Exactly! It hasn't, so let's stick with building your dream and living the life you love.

Strength training: A job is your temporary assignment, not your life assignment.

As mentioned earlier, your job is your temporary assignment, not your life assignment, so let's talk more about this and distinguish the difference between the two.

A temporary assignment is preparation work. School and a job are examples of this. When you go to school, you are in a social setting and a learning environment, so it gives you a greater sense of belonging. You learn communication and relationship building skills; you are feeding your brain with a broader scope of knowledge, hearing perspectives from a diverse community, challenging your ideas and that of others and setting yourself up for new and improved opportunities in a competitive market.

A job offers much the same, in addition to a specific skill-set. You learn by doing (on the job training), you build on your skills as your responsibilities increase, you learn how to work independently and as part of a team. You also participate in a bigger vision and driving results around the company's mission. You need to meet deadlines, facilitate or participate in meetings, speak publicly, learn how to organize and prioritize, make decisions, manage expectations, gain the necessary clerical skills through performing administrative work and have a better understanding of the importance of policies and procedures.

A life assignment is your calling, the real purpose for which you are here, the bigger work you have been selected to do, your life mission. You are the elected individual to bring to this world your unique talent. As so eloquently stated by the one and only Oprah Winfrey, "There is no greater gift you could give or receive than to honor your calling. It's why you were born and how you become most truly alive." There could never be anything that compares to this rewarding and indescribable feeling, and we can assure you that once you realize the reason for your existence and are living the life of your dreams, you won't want to turn back to a mediocre lifestyle that only provided you with the leftovers rather than the overflow.

Stretch and flex: Utilize employable and transferable skills to enter the business world.

Now that you have been well prepared for your temporary assignment, how do you become acclimated to the unknown world of business? What is the best way to get your feet wet? Well, considering everyone is coming from different backgrounds and is at various levels in their personal and professional lives, we can go about this in a few different ways. To ascertain that, we cover the basics of what will apply to most (i.e. the homemakers, the unemployed, those who are role transitioning or took a break from the workforce, as well as those who have been working for years in corporate). We will create a list of skills that will assist in your thinking process. Keep in mind this is not an all-inclusive list, but it will get you started. We will break this down into five categories.

Evidence of transferable skills can be found in the following categories:

1. College Courses
   o Business Management

- ○ Financial Planning and Management
- ○ Communications (e.g. Public Speaking)
- ○ Economics
- ○ Leadership Studies
- ○ Professional Writing
- ○ Psychology
- ○ Professional Development

2. Part-Time/Full-Time Employment

- ○ Time Management
- ○ Office Management
- ○ Delegation Responsibilities
- ○ Multi-Tasking
- ○ Handling Complaints
- ○ Educating and Motivating
- ○ Training and Development
- ○ Coordinating Activities
- ○ Evaluating Work Performance
- ○ Maintaining Records
- ○ Meticulous Attention to Detail (Analytical)

- o Oral and Written Presentation
- o Ability to Handle Crises

3. Volunteer Work
   - o Community Involvement
   - o Tutoring
   - o Daycare or Babysitter/Nanny
   - o Mentoring
   - o Companionship
   - o Running Errands
   - o Counseling
   - o Youth Work
   - o Grass Roots Projects
   - o Administrative/Office Work
   - o Event Planning
   - o Coaching
   - o Charitable Work/Philanthropy
   - o Work in Library
   - o Public Speaking
   - o Non-Profit Work

- o Politics: Help People Register to Vote

- o Summer Camp

- o Collect Clothes, Toys and Food for Donation

- o Work at a Blood Bank

- o Provide Music/Singing, Art, Swimming, or Other Lessons

- o Teach Cooking or Health and Wellness Classes

4. Travel/Vacation Projects

- o Helping a Family in Need

- o Sponsoring a Child

- o Missionary Work (e.g. Education, Hospital)

- o Community Outreach

5. Leisure Activities/Hobbies

- o Create Arts and Crafts

- o Scrapbooking

- o Creative Writing

- o Entertainment: Singing/Dancing/Acting/Spoken Word
- o Gardening
- o Sewing/Knitting/Crocheting
- o Painting
- o Reading Books/Story-Telling
- o Collecting Items
- o Cooking
- o Traveling
- o Language Interpreter
- o Working with Animals

Cool down: Relax and know you got this!

After an intense workout, everything is working overtime. In physical activity, this typically means your heart is beating faster than normal, you're short of breath, your body temperature is raised, and you have worked up a good sweat. In business, your mind is on fast-forward, it may feel like you've just run a marathon or you might feel overworked and overwhelmed. In either case, you need a cooling down period to come down from the physical and mental activity and put you in a relaxed state of mind. Think of it as your recovery period.

Let's start with a brief cool down session that will only take about 5-10 minutes:

First: Sit in a comfortable and quiet place, close your eyes and relax. Now, take in 3-5 slow, deep breaths.

Second: Perform 10 of your favorite stretches, holding each stretch for approximately 10 seconds.

Third: At this moment, be present and think about what you have accomplished just today by staying in action. Let this be an eye-opening experience and a motivator for you to keep going. Now, hold onto your dream and continue to make the decision to gravitate toward it every day.

We trust that you will hold yourself accountable, but teaming up with an accountability partner works well too. You know yourself better than anyone, so this will be your call, but whichever way you decide, know how much you deserve the very best that life has to offer.

CHAPTER 5: New School of Thought: Attention! Class In Session

Hardwired for service excellence.

When we were born, we were already equipped with the necessary tools and resources to excel in life. Our creator aligned our gifts to meet the needs of others, and he prepared the universe to help us deliver the gifts that we were so graciously given. Every fiber of our being was built with wisdom, courage, resilience and endurance, and each of us comes with special features and amenities, which make us unique. Just like a computer is hardwired so it can function properly and perform exceptionally well, that is also true for every individual. We are well connected on the inside so that we can be well connected to the circuits we plug into. When we plug in, others have access to our network. It's the way you are hardwired that will allow you to succeed and outperform beyond any shadow of a doubt you may have. So, you need not worry, or stress, or be fearful about whether or not it can be done. Know that it will be done and all you have to do is plug in and turn the power switch on.

Determine your destiny. Map out the directions to get there.

So how do you accomplish getting from here to there? The first thing you must do is determine your destiny. You already know where you were and where you are now, so the question is: where do you want to be? Do you have a chosen destination, or are you just aimlessly going in whatever direction the wind blows you? You must have a vision and get clear about your destination, so you can map out the directions for getting there. Only then can you determine your destiny and be in control of your destination. You are the author of your story, the captain of your ship, the architect of your blueprint, the CEO of your life, so it is you, as the co-creator, who gets to decide how your future plays out. When you are meeting resistance from others, remind them that you were given a pen and blank pad of paper just as they were. It is not only your right, but it is the expectation that you will create and live by the vision you were blessed to receive and they should be doing the same.

Set your GPS, but use your map as a backup to stay on course.

Thankfully, we no longer need to find monumental landmarks to reference, or laboriously draft out detailed maps, nor do we have to learn how to read a compass, the stars in the night sky, refer to a Thomas Guide or stop by the local gas station and depend on an attendant for directions. We now have a modern device, and it is called a GPS. A global positioning system (GPS) is a constellation of 27 Earth-orbiting satellites, which make up the network that operates as a navigation system. Before the GPS can offer guidance, it needs to know where you are, so that it can navigate you to where you are going. It finds your location and takes you to your destination, which is a thought-provoking concept.

Much the same, you have an internal GPS; you know it as your intuition, your gut feeling. Your internal GPS needs to know your starting point so that it can guide you to your end point. As you travel along your journey, you will be challenged with which direction to take, what is the best route, if you should take any short-cuts and if you are making the right decision. In your situation, that might look like: do I continue to work my full-time job, while pursuing my dream? What is the best way to transition from my current profession to my ideal career? What would happen if I skipped ABC steps to get to XYZ steps… is this the best choice at this time?

No one has a crystal ball or the ability to read the future, so the answers will not always be that obvious. However, you do have your imagination and the ability to picture the outcome of each situation mentally. It's also a good idea to write down the details and weigh out the pros and cons. You will want to do this without distractions, so get to a quiet place and take your time acknowledging your feelings as you go through each scenario. Do you feel uneasy, anxious or short of breath just at the thought of the adjustment you are considering? Or do you feel excited for the opportunity, motivated for change and sold on the idea? This is the process you need to take yourself through because there will always be a fork in the road that challenges your decision-making abilities. You have to be open and willing to trust your decision, and you know better than anybody else what the right decision and right time is for you.

Pay attention to the mile markers as you make headway.

Have you ever taken a long road trip, or even noticed on your route to work, school or other destination that there are signs that have numbers on them, as you travel on the interstate or the local and state highways? Well, those are called mile markers, and they help you determine which direction you're going. As you start to pay attention to the mile markers, you'll notice the numbers either go lower or higher, right? There are several purposes mile markers serve aside from direction: they can be used as a landmark to describe your location in the event you get lost, or your car breaks down. It also serves as a coordinate point, so you know how many miles you've traveled and how many miles more you will need to travel before you reach your destination or the exit that will lead to your destination. For example, if you need to exit on 53 and you've reached mile marker 43, you know you have ten more miles to go, which is something to look forward to. These are considered milestones and they are worth celebrating. So, as you can see, mile markers are very useful for several reasons.

As you travel on your journey to greatness, pay attention to the mile markers you pass. As you make headway toward your destination, applaud yourself and celebrate the incremental steps you are taking to get there. On your way there, you may find yourself tired or exhausted even; pull over and take the rest period necessary to give you just enough rejuvenation, then get back on your path and continue your journey.

Don't let detours discourage you; you will eventually get there.

On our journey, not everything will go smoothly. Sometimes you will run into unpaved or bumpy roads, obstacles will appear out of nowhere, occasionally the white lines are not as clear, and many times there are unexpected detours on the road, and your GPS may not pick up any signals on an unmapped road, or in the area it detoured you to. This can be very frustrating and quite frankly, very scary, especially if it is dark, the roads are quiet, and you are alone. Detours often take you a long, round-about way and, typically, when you need to pull over and ask for some guidance, there is no one around to help. Guess what? You will need to rely on yourself, and you do that by having a backup plan (i.e. a road map). This is a lesson to be learned prior to learning the hard way. Detours are inevitable, especially on con-struction sites where access to main roads is limited; however, you can be prepared for them by having a road map handy. The map should have been highlighted and studied before you started your trip, so you have some idea that you are at least in the vicinity of where you need to be.

Don't panic! If you feel lost, confused or afraid, take some deep breaths to calm yourself, gather your thoughts and, if you are a praying person, prayer works wonders. Regroup, refer to your backup plan, turn on your internal GPS and confidently navigate yourself to a safe zone and continue your path from there. Know this: there is no such thing as the perfect route; you are going to make poor choices and wrong turns. It's not the end of the world; learn from your mistakes, make a better decision next time and keep moving forward. Detours can be discouraging, but you are not in a race. Embrace the learning curve, but slow down because it may be sharp. Although it may be a long journey, you will eventually get there.

CHAPTER 6: What a Transformational Coach and Business Start-up Consultant Can Do for You

What is the role of a business start-up consultant?

Business start-up consultants generally provide services specifically to the start-up companies. They help in selecting the right business idea, the creation of business plans, start-up plans that are in alignment with your life plans, financial projections, investor pitches, pricing, marketing and sales strategies and plans and company & product launching plans.

What is the role of a transformational coach?

A transformational coach, also known as a life coach, assists individuals in figuring out their life plan, especially in times of uncertainty when one's plans did not work out according to how they imagined. Dreams are unique to each individual, so there is no cookie-cutter approach. Transformational coaches help the client gain a new perspective on the way they view themselves and how they respond to inevitable or unforeseen circumstances. They help the client shift limiting beliefs to unlimited possibilities so that they can move forward in prosperity.

You are not alone. Allow us to help.

In addition to the above-described services, we at Shared Visions By CaTwa, provide you with the necessary tools and resources, teach you how to hone your skills and breathe life into your vision, so you can keep it alive and thriving. We give you the boost you need, and you can rest assured that you will never walk away feeling like you have made the wrong decision. We will empower you and welcome you as you make the transition to join in the movement of becoming a "visionette," a part of our tribe.

So, as we bring our conversation to a close, we want to thank you for taking the time to pickup our book and read our special message to you. There are many books to choose from, but this book, in particular, was the one chosen for you. So many people spend a lifetime trying to figure out what you already know. What am I here for? You no longer have to ask that question because you now have some answers or at least a starting point in how to get there. Now, you can apply what you've learned to get your life back on track, and you can also gift a friend, a loved one, or a colleague with this message, so they can stop searching for the very thing that lies within them, waiting patiently to be discovered.

Once again, we congratulate you for making the decision to take control of your life, realizing that you are enough as you are and there is not another you anywhere in this world who can do what you do, in a way that only you can do. Take pride in knowing that, stay true to you, keep the faith, trust the process and know in your heart of hearts, you are worth the investment and entitled to a life of fulfillment. Don't short-change yourself. Stop accepting the leftovers and neglecting your needs because at the end of the day, when it's just you and your thoughts behind closed doors, in the still, calm, quiet of the night with no interruptions and no distractions, your rest does not come easy as you reflect on your life, wondering, hoping, or wishing about what has been versus what could be. You know, like nobody else, that you deserve so much more than the hand you've been dealt, yet you lie silent, motionless, betraying and resisting your truth, holding onto the lies that continue to deceive you as you watch the years pass by.

Look at where you are today. Realize that all the things you've been through and the life that you had was no accident. There is a way to change tomorrow, and it all comes from embracing you. There is no expiration on your dreams except for the one that you've put there. So our question for you is: What is your untold story? Are you going to continue to live with the regret? Are you headed toward dying with your dreams or are you ready to choose to walk in your awesomeness?

Don't be the person that lives in hiding or the one who buries her dreams. Be the one who rescues herself from what could have, would have or should have been; be the one who chooses, with all that you are, to walk in your awesomeness at any age, today and every day because dreams don't expire until you do.

It is our hope that we have been informative, inspiring, motivating, empowering and perhaps a little humorous. Remember: Those who sell themselves anything short of the miracle that lies dormant within them will not have lived at all, but will have robbed themselves and the world of a gift that was never known.

Wholeheartedly in this journey with you,

~ Catrina and Twana ~

Invitation to Work with Us

Although our message to you has come to an end in the pages of this book, our journey together has just begun. We have developed signature programs that will allow us to work together far beyond the words of this book. It is imperative that you get the education, guidance, and support necessary to help you succeed in your business and in your life. Just as a Personal Fitness Trainer works with you to create a customized action plan that is unique to your individual needs, pushes you past your comfort zone so you can see results, holds you accountable, gives you honest feedback and reminds you to celebrate your wins, Coaches and Consultants are Personal Mentors who have your best interest at heart and will do the same. In fact, we believe in the power of Personal Business Mentors so much that we have invested in more than one and it has been life-changing! As we have repeatedly said throughout our book, it doesn't matter where you are starting from; the key is to get started. Everyone must start somewhere, so why not start here, today and transform your life and invite others to join you in the journey! This is an excellent way to kick off the New Year and is the gift of a lifetime!

If you are still uncertain about an Entrepreneurial Consultant or Transformational Coach being right for you, ask yourself these questions, answer them honestly and decide for yourself:

- Are YOU TIRED of working your nine to five and building someone else's dream?
- Do you have BIG Goals, BIG Dreams and BIG Visions and know you are here for something greater, but you lack the HOW TO?
- Do you feel that you are OVER THE AGE LIMIT to pursue your dreams?
- Are you READY to start a PASSION-filled, PURPOSE-driven business, one that is in alignment with the truth of who you are, but you don't know the next steps to take?

- How long has this battle inside of you gone on and kept you awake at night?
- Will you allow time to keep passing by, or will you take action and take your life back?
- Is your FEAR stronger than your FAITH?

YOU ARE THE AUTHOR OF YOUR STORY AND LIFE IS ABOUT CHOICES.

YOU OWE IT TO YOU TO INVEST IN YOURSELF AND YOU CAN "WALK IN YOUR AWESOMENESS" AT ANY AGE WITHOUT PERMISSION!

Collectively, Women are in this struggle together. Without realizing it, we self-sabotage the life we are deserving of because we spend an excess amount of time convincing ourselves of negative self-talk; We get in our own way.

We live in a BRAINWASHED society that teaches us one path to success. . .

Go to school, graduate with a diploma, get a higher education and obtain a degree, land your "dream job" in Corporate America, climb the ladder, retire well and live happily ever after. Yet, we are not given a backup plan for how to succeed WHEN this FAIRYTALE turns into a NIGHTMARE ~ When we end up with DEBT, a DEAD-END job, LAID OFF, UN-EMPLOYED. . .Back to the STRUGGLE.

WE understand how you feel because WE have walked in your shoes.

We have worked in Corporate America for 30 years, while we knowingly deferred our dreams. Why? Because it was a FAMILIAR place to be, a COMFORTABLE routine, it provided for our livelihood, and it offered a FALSE SENSE OF SECURITY, BUT. . . At the end of the day, we were UNHAPPY, and it was an UN-HEALTHY cycle of dissatisfaction to feel IM-MOBILE in an UNSTABLE environment.

The juggling act of working a nine to five, sometimes two to make ends meet, "Robbing Peter to Pay Paul," the demands of life, the responsibilities of caring for your family and household, going back to school to better your chances of getting a more promising job, working your business as a side hustle and feeling burned out. This is not LIVING; this is BARELY SURVIVING!

Ladies ~ A TRADITIONAL career path is an old school of thought.
ENTREPRENEURSHIP is the new movement!

Once we realized we were allowing ourselves to be incarcerated by a system that is set-up to keep us dependent on it and addicted to it, we decided to get smart and invest our time, energy and hard-earned money into ourselves. You too CAN and SHOULD create your own opportunities and wealth and STOP making someone else wealthy off your talents, sweat and years of loyalty. It doesn't have to be this way. You and your family deserve more than a mediocre life.

We know change can be UNCOMFORTA-BLE and stepping out on faith can be SCARY, but you don't have to do it ALONE. We are here for you. BUT. . .You do need to have a VISION, be willing to SHARE YOUR

STORY and BELIEVE that you can ACHIEVE anything your heart desires. We have learned how to transition from CORPORATE AMERICA into the WORLD OF BUSINESS without disrupting our lifestyle. There is so MUCH MORE to life than being stuck behind a desk or cubicle, surrounded by office politics and negative energy, feeling ENSLAVED and ENTRAPPED. It all starts by making a different CHOICE and changing your MINDSET. No One is EXEMPT from ABUNDANCE!

FACTS: Research shows that women have been starting businesses at a higher rate than men for the last 20 years and tend to create home-based micro (less than five employees) and small businesses. Women will create over half of the 9.72 million new small business jobs expected to be created by 2018, and more and more are doing this from home offices across the country, (Forbes). Furthermore, in-depth studies have shared insight on the subject, and what they have found to be consistent across the board is that starting a business has been at an all-time high and women crave control over their lives and overall fulfillment.

We INVITE you to reach out to us for help. Don't be too proud to ASK. We will start with a COMPLIMENTARY Discovery Session. Next, we will help you BREAKTHROUGH your challenges; Then, we will help you CONNECT your PASSION to your PURPOSE, and construct a business based on AUTHENTICITY; Let us EDUCATE, GUIDE and SUPPORT you during your transformation.

BECOME A "VISIONETTE" AND JOIN THE MOVEMENT!

Take a moment to evaluate your commitment and readiness level:

This IS for WOMEN who are ready to:

- Commit to yourself and change your current circumstances

- Create fortunes from your misfortunes and expect great things to happen

- Be open to receive education, guidance, and support from experienced professionals

- Change your conditioned mindset and learn a new school of thought

- Understand the power of your message and share your story with others

- Accept gentle challenges that will propel you forward and keep you in action

- Let your light shine brightly and leverage social media

- Put some "skin in" by investing time, energy and finances to get to your next level

- Know your worth, OWN your truth and Embrace your power

- Create endless possibilities for yourself and solidify your legacy

This is NOT for Women who:

- Are looking for an overnight success story

- Need approval or permission to do what is best for them

- Are not ready to stay the course and be consistent

- Are more afraid than they are brave enough to at least make their best effort

- Are not ready to hear the truth so that they can make the necessary changes

- Are not willing to do whatever is necessary to succeed

- Are not teachable and feel that they are satisfied with where they are

- Come with excessive emotional baggage and need extra hand-holding

- Don't have the motivation and ambition to do the work required

WHAT YOU CAN EXPECT:

We will take the opportunity to review every application we receive; however, the Discovery Session is for women seriously considering working with us. During our call, this is an opportunity for us to get better acquainted. We will have an open dialogue and questions are strongly encouraged. Your information will be held in the strictest of confidence, as we highly respect your privacy.

The time you spend with us on the Discovery Session will:

- Be an eye-opening, breakthrough experience
- Immediately help you identify your challenges
- Provide some insight as to why you are struggling
- Give you clarity on your message or story
- Get you better organized on your priorities
- Help you set realistic goals and action steps

As a part of our screening process, we reserve the right to determine if we are a good fit for one another. If we mutually agree we are an ideal match, we will decide at that time which one of our programs you qualify for and would be most effective for you. You have already taken the FIRST STEP by reading our book and you have come to the right place.

The next step is to TYPE THE LINK BELOW into your web browser, complete the application process and SCHEDULE a COMPLIMENTARY Discovery Session with us: https://sharedvisionsbycatwa.acuityscheduling.com/

Feel free to visit our website at http://www.SharedVisionsByCaTwa.com/ to learn more about us and check back frequently for updates.

We feel very honored to be in a position to work with wonderful women from all walks of life and IF you have decided to move forward, you are making a smart decision and investment to work closely with coaches who will help you expedite your progress and watch you excel. What an AMAZING opportunity you have been presented with and we are thoroughly excited for you! It is a rewarding feeling for us, just as much as it is for you, to watch your life transform.
ENVISION THE POSSIBILITIES. . .

~ Wholeheartedly in this Journey with You~Catrina and Twana

About the Authors

Catrina M. Wilson (formerly Crowel), from San Diego, California and Twana Y. Wilson, from Queens, New York, currently reside in Atlanta, Georgia and are known as the dynamic duo and founders of Shared Visions By CaTwa! They are highly-regarded, well-respected Authors, Speakers, Entrepreneurial Consultants and Transformational Coaches, specializing in women-owned and operated start-up and small businesses. With a professional and educational background in start-up management, organizational leadership, business operations, advisory, mentorship, psychology and 30 years in Corporate America, they are influential leaders and catalysts for change surrounding limiting beliefs that paralyze progress. They believe conditioned minds are developed in a brainwashed society and re-programming the mind to buy into a new school of thought will demonstrate how success can be achieved beyond current circumstances.